Stuck in Bed

The pregnancy bed rest picture book for kids...
and moms

Written by Jennifer Degl and Angela Davids

Illustrations by Jennifer Lynn Becker

Lemon Tree Publishing

www.StuckInBedBook.com

ISBN-13: 978-0692091142
ISBN-10: 0692091149

Printed in the United States of America
First Printing 2018

Limits of Liability/Disclaimer: The authors have shared their unique experiences with being on pregnancy bed rest. The tips provided in this book are strictly for informational purposes and are not intended as a substitute for the medical advice of health care providers. The reader assumes all responsibility and liability for the use of the information contained herein.

I dedicate this book to my husband and four children, for their support and endurance — but especially to my Shane. While I was on bed rest and while your sister spent four months in the NICU, you were a very brave big boy, and I will always be proud of you.

— Jennifer Degl

I dedicate this book to my very patient husband and our two bed rest kids. I am eternally grateful for the support I had from my family during fifteen weeks of bed rest with my second pregnancy, especially the support from Marilee, Melissa and Joanna.

— Angela Davids

Dear moms,

No one expects to have a high-risk pregnancy, but it can happen to anyone. Pregnancy can be an emotional time, even when everything is going well. Then being told that you have to restrict your activity or go on bed rest can bring out new emotions, like anxiety and frustration. It can seem impossible to accept that this is temporary, but it is just that — temporary. Of the moments that make up your life, these are only a few.

We wrote this book to help guide you on your journey through pregnancy bed rest, so that you can learn how to enjoy this time in your life, despite your doctor's orders. We've both been there and we understand, and we want to help. We wish you the best of luck on your journey!

— Jennifer Degl and Angela Davids

"We have great news," my parents said

"Come over here and sit on the bed."

"We're having a baby," my mommy said.

I got so excited that my face
turned
RED!

TIP! **Although you may be having concerns about the future of your pregnancy, try to stay positive around your child. Every child reacts differently to a pregnancy announcement, from excitement to jealousy to indifference, so don't read too much into their response.**

"Tell me when!   Tell me when!"

I excitedly said.

"Not just yet. It's a few months ahead."

TIP! **For moms on bed rest, there's a sense of accomplishment as you get through each day. Have your child draw an X on the calendar for you, or pull off the top sheet of a stack of sticky notes where you have written the number of days until your due date.**

"And now Mommy has to stay here in her bed."

"Why is that?" I asked, as I tilted my head.

"Do you have yucky germs

that you could spread?"

"No, the baby just needs me to rest,"

she said.

TIP! **Other positive statements you can make are: "When I stay in bed, it helps the baby to grow." "When I lay down, it makes the baby happy."**

8

"But it's winter now,

and who will pull my sled?"

"Daddy can do it, or Uncle Ted."

"At breakfast time,

who will toast my bread?"

"Grandma or Grandpa can do it instead."

TIP! **Ask your child if there are "big boy" or "big girl" things they would want to do, like getting dressed on their own, putting a sippy cup in the sink, or bringing Mommy a snack.**

"But I want Mommy!" I *pled* and *pled*.

"We will sing and play games

and put toys in the bed."

TIP! *Choose some activities that your child does only with you to make your time together special: reading certain books, making simple crafts, or playing educational games on a tablet or laptop.*

"I can promise you now that your books
                                        will be read.

We could quilt the baby a blanket with
                                        needles and thread."

 TIP! *Encourage your child to talk to your baby and describe what he or she sees and feels. Throughout your pregnancy, ask your child what he or she is looking forward to as a big brother or sister.*

"And I don't even mind if you eat snacks
in my bed."

"This might be fun," said a voice in my head.

 It will be difficult to do from bed, but try to maintain a routine for your child. It can be reassuring, and it will help their days go by quickly.

"It won't always be easy," my mommy said.

"But it won't last forever,
                me stuck in this bed."

 Bed rest can be difficult for kids and it is never easy for moms. Search for online support groups where you can connect with other women on bed rest or who are having a high-risk pregnancy.

"I love you so very much," my mommy said.

"We'll get really good at snuggling,
                            here in my bed!"

TIP! **Also tell your partner how much you love them and appreciate them. They may be overwhelmed with their additional responsibilities, or they might feel helpless about what they can do for the baby. Make time to connect.**

Then once the baby came,
no more tears were shed.

And sometimes I miss those days,
being stuck in Mommy's bed.

TIP! **Children can be surprisingly resilient and adaptable, so don't be too hard on yourself or feel guilty over the things that you can't do for them right now. By doing all you can to keep your unborn baby safe, you're making a difference for your entire family.**

Use the space below to write a letter to your child or children who are on the bed rest journey along with you. You can write about the fun things you will do together during this time, or write about the things you will do when the new baby gets here.

About the Illustrator

Jennifer Lynn Becker is a professional artist and illustrator living in South Central Pennsylvania with a few cats and a lot of plants. Her focus is on illustrating children's books as well as botanical artworks that highlight environmental concerns and solutions. She works in a variety of media, including pastel, watercolor, and graphite. You can see her artwork on her website, *www.jenbecker.com*.

Use the space below to write a message to your bed rest baby (or babies) to read in the years ahead.

About the Authors

Jennifer Degl is the founder of *Speaking for Moms & Babies, Inc.*, which advocates for maternal and neonatal health by sharing the parent voice, and is the author of another book called *From Hope to Joy: A Memoir of a Mother's Determination and Her Micro Preemie's Struggle to Beat the Odds*. She endured 6 weeks of both home and hospital bed rest, due to a life-threatening case of placenta accreta, while her youngest child was just 3 years old and he had a difficult time understanding what was going on. Jennifer and her premature baby survived this pregnancy and she now wants to help others who are struggling with high-risk pregnancies and premature births. Jennifer is a high school science teacher by day and lives in New York with her husband and four children. To learn more, please visit *SpeakingForMomsAndBabies.com*.

Angela Davids is the creator of *KeepEmCookin.com*, an educational website and online support group for women who are experiencing a high-risk pregnancy or who are at risk of delivering prematurely. She spent a total of 21 weeks on bedrest during her two pregnancies. She faced multiple complications, but ultimately delivered her daughter at 39 weeks and her son at 39 weeks and 3 days. Her favorite part of running *KeepEmCookin.com* is reading the many success stories she hears from members. She can say with confidence, "Anything is possible."

Made in the USA
Columbia, SC
02 March 2019